Discovering
What
Frogs
Do

Illustrated by
Jean Zallinger

Discovering
What
Frogs
Do

by Seymour Simon

McGRAW-HILL BOOK COMPANY

New York • St. Louis • San Francisco • Toronto
London • Sydney • Mexico • Panama

For Joyce, Robbie, and Mike

Library of Congress Catalog Card Number: 77-88330

1234567890 HDEC 754321069

Contents

1

How To Be
A Frog Watcher

Early spring is the best time to be on the look-out for frogs. One of the first kinds of frogs to come out of its long winter sleep is the leopard frog. By the beginning of April, you can often hear a chorus of croaking leopard frogs around slowly warming ponds and streams.

Leopard frogs spend the winter in the mud at the bottom of ponds or under logs and stones in streams. The lengthening hours of sunlight in spring and the slowly rising temperature of the water stirs the frogs into action.

Springtime is the leopard frogs' breeding season. This is the only time during the year that the adult frogs gather in large groups. In the early evening, one of the male frogs begins to croak—a low, hoarse *ker-r-r-ock, ker-r-r-ock*. As if waiting for the signal, the other male frogs join in the chorus. Now the noise is loud and steady. You can hear it from a mile off on a quiet night.

The frogs also croak during the day, but their chorus is not as noisy because fewer croak then. When you come upon frogs in a pond, the chorus suddenly stops. The water looks still and deserted. Be quiet for a while. If you can, crouch behind a tree or a bush.

After a few minutes you may spot the frogs sitting (half-submerged) on the shallow edges of the pond. Leopard frogs are green, with darker spots ringed with white. They are pure white underneath. They look streamlined and speedy when jumping or swimming.

Soon you will hear one frog begin to croak, then another, and another. Only male frogs croak during the breeding season.

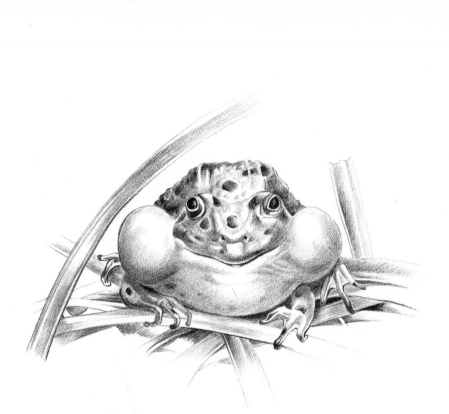

Each frog takes a big breath of air before it croaks. Swellings appear on either side between its mouth and shoulder. These are the vocal sacs. The croaking sounds are made by vibrations of the vocal cords. The sacs reinforce the sound and make it louder. The croaking grows louder and louder. All of a sudden it stops, and the swellings collapse like deflated balloons.

During July and August, thousands of young leopard frogs ring the shores of the ponds in which they hatched. Later in the summer, most of them may be found hopping around damp spots in meadows and fields. Other common kinds of frogs that you might see around ponds or damp places are pickerel frogs, green frogs, and bull frogs.

2

Collecting and Keeping Frogs

You can probably find frogs around water during most of the warmer months of the year. But spring-time is when you will find frogs clustered together in the greatest numbers.

It's best to take a long-handled net with you when you go collecting. It's possible to catch a frog with your hands, but a net makes the job much easier.

A small aquarium net for lifting frogs' eggs, a widemouthed jar or two, and a notebook and pencil, are all the other materials you need for your frog-

hunting expedition. The notebook is to record what you see on the spot before you forget it. Also write down questions that you find puzzling. You may find some of the answers in later observations that you make.

Frogs face the water when they sit at the edge of a pond or stream. If you approach slowly and make no sudden movements you may get close enough to capture a basking frog. Quickly place your net in front of the frog. The motion will make him leap forward. But if you stumble upon a hidden frog, you will know about it by a splash in the water. Frogs only make splashes when they suddenly jump to flee an enemy. If you watch frogs without disturbing them, you will see that they usually slip into the water quietly.

Catch and keep only those frogs that you are prepared to care for at home. Two frogs are enough for a ten-gallon aquarium. If you catch a mating pair clasped together, place them in your aquarium and they may lay their eggs. You can carry the frogs home in a covered widemouthed jar containing a little pond water or some moist leaves. Be sure to punch some air holes in the cover so that the jagged edges point outward. Frogs can also be brought home in a small cloth bag dampened with water. Do not leave either container in direct sunlight or near a warm radiator.

Use the smaller net to dip up some eggs for home observation. A dozen eggs are enough. If you keep too many eggs in a small aquarium, they will all die. Catch several tadpoles and carry them in the same jar as the eggs. Half fill the jar with water. You can also add a few green plants growing in the pond such as Elodea or duckweed.

At home, eggs can be kept in almost any clean container, except a metal one. You can use a small aquarium, a widemouthed glass jar, a plastic container, or even a soup dish. Keep the eggs in the pond water you collected. Keep the water out of direct sunlight and away from heat. Change the water every week with some fresh pond water or some tap water that has been allowed to stand for twenty-four hours.

Tadpoles can also be kept in a small aquarium or in a widemouthed jar. Keep only three or four tadpoles in each gallon of water to prevent overcrowding. Tadpoles eat plant material and there should be a constant supply for them. If there are not enough plants in the aquarium, add a small piece of boiled lettuce or spinach.

Adult frogs should be kept in a separate aquarium. Place about two or three inches of water in a ten-gallon or larger aquarium. Build up one end of the aquarium with gravel and small rocks. This will allow the frogs a chance to swim as well as to rest. Screen the top to prevent the frogs from jumping out. It's a good idea to siphon off the water and replace it with fresh water every other week.

Make sure that the aquarium is not in direct sunlight for any length of time. The temperature in the aquarium could become very high and the frogs would probably die. Of course, there should always be water kept in the tank. A dry frog will die in a short time.

Frogs need to be fed. They will snap at any small moving insect. But they will not eat any food, no matter what, if it is not in motion. One scientist fed frogs for months with living, moving mealworms. Yet he found that frogs did not snap at motionless mealworms, regardless of how hungry they were. In fact, a frog can starve to death in the middle of piles of food unless the food moves.

15

Feed your frogs small insects, mealworms, spiders, even earthworms if the frogs are large enough to eat them. Also try feeding them bits of scraped lean meat. Stick a bit of meat on a long thread and dangle it in front of a frog. Make sure your hand is out of sight. Frogs will snap at any small moving object.

Keeping frogs over the winter is a different matter. Frogs go into a winter sleep during cold weather (see page 39). You can keep them in an aquarium. Supply some soil and leaves for the frogs to burrow under. Keep the aquarium in a cool place, but not where it will freeze solid. Ever so often, sprinkle water over the leaves and soil to keep the frogs moist. Perhaps the best thing to do is to release frogs in autumn before the first frost, and catch new ones the following spring.

When you pick up a frog, hold it gently by its body and not by its hind legs. Holding it by the legs could injure the frog if it tried to jump away. When you keep an animal at home, you are responsible for its health and well-being. When you no longer want it, release it in its natural surroundings.

16

3

The Outside and Inside of a Frog

Frogs do not have scales as do fish, feathers as do birds, or hair as do mammals. Frogs are *amphibians,* taken from a Greek word meaning living a double life. The double life of frogs includes the water-living stage of tadpoles and the land-living stage of adult frogs.

How does a frog breathe underwater? The answer lies in the frog's skin. The skin is very thin and contains many blood vessels. When a frog is underwater, dissolved oxygen from air in the water passes through its skin into its bloodstream. A waste gas, carbon dioxide, passes out through the frog's skin into the water.

When a frog is not very active, it gets air through its skin. But swimming or being in a warm temperature increases a frog's air needs. Then the frog must come to the surface to breath.

Look at the frog's bulging eyes. When a frog floats just below the surface, its eyes, like the periscope of a submarine, are on the lookout above the

water. Its body is well camouflaged and is difficult to see from above or below.

Look for a lower eyelid covering the eye. This eyelid is transparent. It helps protect the eye underwater and keeps it moist on land. Touch this eyelid lightly and the frog will respond by drawing the eyelid over the eye and pulling the eye back into the head.

A frog does not have ears on the outside of its body as you do. Its eardrums are level with the surface of the skin. Don't confuse the eardrums with the large round circles found under the eyes in some leopard frogs. These are the male leopard frog's vocal sacs.

The frog's nostrils are back toward the top of its head. This allows the frog to breathe air when floating with most of its body submerged. What advantage is there for the frog in being able to breathe with most of its body below water?

A frog's mouth is very large. It has to be. It's used as an insect catcher. The frog's sticky tongue is attached to the front of the jaw rather than to the back. This allows it to move far outside the mouth.

Try to watch a frog catch an insect. The action is so fast that you can hardly see it. If you could watch in slow motion, you would see the mouth open wide and the tongue flip out and over. The insect is caught on the tongue's sticky surface and is flipped back into the mouth. The eyelids blink, and the insect is swallowed. The frog doesn't even chew its food.

In the back of the frog's mouth are two openings. One leads to the food tube. The other is the opening to the lungs. The small round teeth on the upper jaw help the frog to hold any larger animals it may catch.

The front legs of a frog are short and not very strong. They have four toes and no webbing. Watch a frog swimming and you will see that it doesn't use its front legs very much in the water. But if you place a frog on the ground and watch it jump, you will see that it lands on its front legs. A frog also uses its front legs to prop up its body when sitting.

The hind legs are the power legs. They are folded against the body when a frog is resting. When the frog jumps, it pushes off with its powerful hind legs.

Try measuring how far your frog can jump. Is it a good jumper? At the Calaveras County Fair in California, a Frog Olympic Jumping Contest is held. Several hundred dollars in prizes are awarded. But don't get your hopes up too high. Some foreign frogs can jump well over ten feet!

Place your frog in some water and watch how it uses its hind legs to swim. Naturally, it does the "frog kick" when swimming. The hind legs fold up, then stretch far out. Five long toes on each foot stretch out the webbing between them. The feet act like paddles pushing against the water. Can you see why we use the name "frogmen" for certain divers?

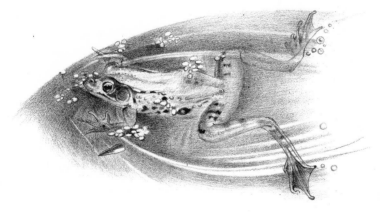

A frog digests its food like other animals with backbones. It has a long food tube through which the food passes to the stomach, the small intestine, and the large intestine. Here the food is mixed with digestive juices. The digestive juices change the food into a form in which it can be used by the body. Undigested food collects in the lower part of the large intestine called the cloaca. The wastes are then excreted from the body through the anal opening.

A frog has a three-chambered heart that pumps blood through blood vessels in its body. Blood carries digested food and other materials. The heart receives blood from the body in one of the chambers and blood from the lungs in another chamber.

The blood returning from the body contains carbon dioxide and other cell wastes. The blood returning from the lungs contains the needed gas, oxygen. Both kinds of blood are mixed together in the third chamber. This chamber pumps blood back to all parts of the body, including the lungs.

4

Egg to Tadpole to Frog

Leopard frogs come out of their winter sleep early in the spring. But the temperature of the water must be at least 41° Fahrenheit before the female frog can lay her eggs. This usually happens sometime between the end of March and the middle of May.

During the breeding season, the male leopard frogs croak while the females are usually silent. The frogs call when floating in water. The male leopard frog clasps a female before the eggs are laid. The eggs pass out of the cloaca of the female directly into the water. The male spreads sperm cells over them. The sperm cells unite with the eggs fertilizing them.

The eggs are laid in clumps of several hundred attached to water plants. One female may lay as many as 4,500 eggs. Each egg is less than a tenth of an inch across and looks like a small black bead. The egg is surrounded by two coats of a jellylike material. This swells up in the water and joins the eggs together in large clumps.

Look at one of the eggs more closely. Use a mag-

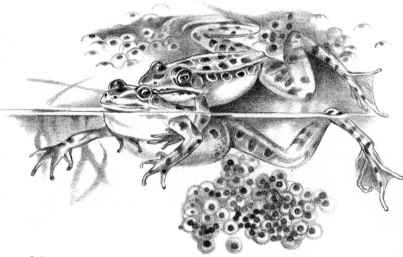

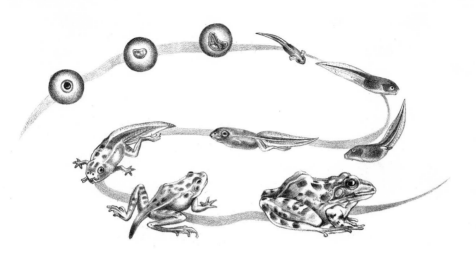

nifying glass if you can. The egg is black above and white below. The white part is the yolk. It contains stored food material, which will be used by the growing tadpole. The dark part is the developing young.

The white yolk is the heavier part, so that the egg floats dark side up. The dark side is warmed by the sun, while the white side makes the egg difficult to see from below. How is this an advantage for the egg?

In natural surroundings, it takes from about eight to twenty days for the eggs to hatch. But they will hatch more quickly if you keep them in a warm house.

Here's an experiment you can do to see how temperature affects the hatching time. Place several eggs and some pond water into three clean wide-mouthed jars. Keep one of the jars at room temperature. Place one of the jars in your refrigerator (not the freezer part). Place the other jar outside your window.

Each day check the temperature of the water in the jars and observe the development of the eggs. Remove any dead eggs or any tadpoles as soon as they hatch. Some experiments show that at 68° Fahrenheit the eggs hatch in four days. How do your results compare with this? Do you think that different amounts of daylight may affect hatching? How could you set up an experiment to test for this?

After an egg hatches, a tadpole wiggles away from the egg mass and attaches itself to a plant. Just after hatching, a tadpole is a tiny, flat animal. It has no mouth, nostrils, or legs. If you use a magnifying glass, you will see that it attaches itself to the plant by two sticky cups.

For the first few days, the tadpole spends most of its time attached to plants, egg jelly, or other objects around it. It is feeding on its own yolk. During this time, its tail grows larger, and external (outside) gills form with which the tadpole obtains oxygen from the water, like a fish.

Now the tadpole begins to swim freely from plant to plant. Its mouth opens and it begins to feed. You may have to add food from time to time. (see page 14).

As the tadpole grows, its internal (inside) gills grow, and the outside ones disappear. At this time, you can see the tadpole open and close its mouth. Can you guess why it is doing this? It is taking in water and passing it over its inside gills. The water then flows out through an opening on each side of its head.

During the next two to three months, a great change takes place in the leopard frog tadpole. Small hind legs appear and begin to grow larger. Toes form and the legs thicken. Soon they begin to look like frog's legs. The tadpole begins to use the legs to help in swimming.

After the hind legs are developed, the front legs appear. As soon as they appear, the tail begins to grow shorter. The body changes shape. The tadpole begins looking like a frog. Inside the tadpole, lungs are developing. The inside gills disappear. The tadpole begins to surface for a breath of air. Place a few rocks in the aquarium at this time, so that the tadpoles can rest on them while breathing air. Otherwise they might drown.

About this time, you can begin feeding the young tadpole-frog small water animals such as Daphnia (small-sized relatives of a lobster) or bits of meat. Almost any kind of moving animal food will be eaten if it is small enough to be swallowed. If you cannot feed your frog, return it to the pond.

After a while, the tail is completely gone. In place of a tadpole, you have a complete tiny frog. The tadpole-frog becomes a one-inch adult frog in about one month. In nature, adult leopard frogs of from one to three or four inches in length usually appear about July.

5

How Do Frogs Sense The World Around Them?

Frogs sense their surroundings with organs such as their eyes, ears, and skin. Sense organs contain special kinds of nerve cells. Each kind of nerve cell is sensitive to a particular message. Some nerve cells are sensitive to touch, others to light, still others to sound, and so on.

You can learn about a frog's senses by doing several simple experiments. For example, touch a frog's skin with a pencil or your finger. The frog will usually respond by jumping. But, if you continue to touch its skin, after a while the frog will no longer respond. If you now dip the pencil into a weak acid such as vinegar and touch the frog, it will probably jump again. After it responds to the vinegar, wash it off. Its skin is sensitive not only to touch, but to certain chemicals as well.

The ability to sense chemicals is also present in a frog's mouth. The taste of certain insects, such as acid-producing red ants, makes the frog get rid of the object quickly. Put some vinegar on a mealworm and feed it to a frog. What do you think will happen?

Frogs sense light and respond to it in many dif-

ferent ways. They will usually try to move away from a very strong light. But once away from the strong light, they may turn around and face toward it. Yet this is not always so. Temperature, hunger, and other conditions seem to influence the way the frog responds.

Experiments have shown that some kinds of frogs have skins that are sensitive to light. One scientist found that blind frogs still turned and jumped toward light.

Certain kinds of frogs seem to prefer green or blue light to other colors. You might try an experiment with your frogs by placing a green or blue light above one corner of their aquarium and a red light above another corner. Observe the frogs for several days and keep a record of which corner they are in each time you look. Do the frogs seem to prefer one kind of light over the other?

Switch the position of the lights and observe for several more days. What are your results now? Why does switching the lights help rule out other conditions in the aquarium such as temperature differences? Certain frogs look for food in green grass, rather than along the banks of a pond. Might this be related to the color of light they seem to prefer?

A frog will snap at any small moving object that it sees. Size and movement seem to be important here. You can experiment with this response by presenting the frog with small and large bits of meat dangled on a string (see page 16). Is there a size so large that the frog will not snap at it? Of what advantage is this response to the frog?

In the field, you can see how quickly frogs respond to the sight of a large moving object. A chorus of frogs will usually stop croaking when they see you moving toward them. On the other hand, if you remain hidden from them, you can often make noises without stopping their croaking. Vision is probably the frog's most important sense.

Hearing is another important sense for frogs. The croaking choruses of frogs each spring are one proof of that. Male frogs attract female frogs by croaking. A male frog seizes the first female to come near him. Sometimes by chance, a male frog clasps another male frog instead of a female. The second male croaks, and this signals the first male away.

A male frog kept in an aquarium during the spring will sometimes croak at the sound of splashing water. Yet other sounds such as your voice will not have this effect. Also try to make a frog croak by rubbing its sides.

Borrow a record of frog sounds at your library or record the croaking of frogs on a tape recorder. Play these back to a male frog in your aquarium. Does he respond by croaking himself? Does he respond to the croaking of other frogs or only his own kind? What do you think will happen?

Frogs are sensitive to many other things. Some kinds respond to water currents by swimming against the current. Some can locate food by smell. Some move into places where their bodies are in contact with a solid object. This results in their burrowing under rocks or logs.

Keep records of what you find out about the senses of frogs. Share your findings with your friends or classmates. Perhaps they can help you to do some of the experiments. You may enjoy giving a report of your findings to a science club or at a science fair.

6

Can Frogs Learn?

There is a very easy experiment you can do to show that frogs can learn. Just feed your frogs on a regular schedule. After several weeks the frogs will turn toward you, when you approach their aquarium. They seem to be waiting expectantly to be fed.

Frogs can learn to avoid certain types of food as well. One scientist gave a frog a hairy caterpillar to eat. A hairy caterpillar is very spiky and makes poor food for a frog. At first, the frog snapped up the caterpillar and then spat it out. But after several more trials, the frog changed its behavior. The frog would approach the caterpillar. It would put out its tongue slowly and just touch the spiky hairs. Then it would withdraw its tongue and take no further action. The frog had learned not to snap at that kind of food.

You can try the same experiment if you can find some hairy caterpillars. If you can't find any, try making an unpleasant tasting food by dipping it in vinegar and presenting it to the frog. You might use a mealworm for this experiment. Give the vinegar-dipped mealworm to the frog at intervals of five minutes. Does the frog learn to avoid the food? Try giv-

ing a mealworm to the frog the next day. Does the frog remember not to snap?

In some ways it is hard for a frog to learn not to snap at food. Put a moving insect behind a pane of glass and show it to a frog. The frog will probably continue to snap at the insect even after many unsuccessful attempts. It also seems impossible to train a frog to snap at a nonmoving insect (see page 15).

You can try a simple experiment to test a frog's ability to learn. Set up a box with a plate of glass as shown in the drawing. Use an earthworm or meal-worm as a reward.

Start the frog at one end of the box. Note that the frog has to jump around the glass to get at the worm. It may take the frog many trials to learn not to bump into the glass. Keep a record of its attempts to see if any progress is made.

In nature, frogs have been found to be able to return to their own pond from distances up to one quarter of a mile. Even obstacles and other ponds in between don't seem to prevent their return.

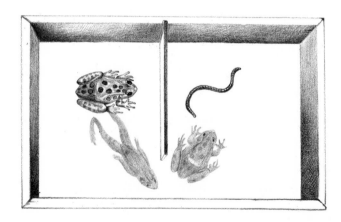

7

~~~~~~

Frogs In Winter

By early autumn, leopard frogs begin to appear around the edges of brooks and ponds. Days grow shorter and temperatures begin to drop. By October or November at the latest, each leopard frog has nosed its way into water and settled to the bottom. Many squirm their way into the soft mud bottom. Others find places under rocks or logs. Here they will remain in hibernation until spring.

Frogs can live under water at temperatures close to freezing for long periods of time. Yet they would die if they spent the winter on land. A leopard frog cannot survive temperatures below freezing. If a frog is frozen solid during the winter, it will not live.

You can experiment to observe what happens when a frog goes into hibernation. You will need a widemouthed jar or a small aquarium a screen covering, water, a flat pan or dish, ice cubes, and a thermometer. Place several inches of water in the jar. Put a leopard frog in the jar and cover it with a wire screen. Place the jar in a pan of ice cubes. Heap more ice cubes around the jar.

When the water temperature drops to 50° Fahrenheit, the frog will swim downward and sprawl on the bottom. If you place an object in the jar, the frog will try to burrow under it, just as it does in nature. If you touch the frog, it will not respond quickly. If one part of the jar is kept darker than the other part, the frog will move so as to stay in the dark part. In warmer water, the frog will usually move toward the light.

If the water remains at this temperature, the frog will return to the surface after a time. When its head is above the water, watch the underside of the

40

frog's mouth and you can count the number of breathing movements it makes. What happens to the number of breathing movements as the temperature drops?

When the temperature goes down to about 40° Fahrenheit, the frog settles on the bottom and remains there. During hibernation, the frog's eyes are covered by the transparent lower eyelid. Its legs and arms are stiffly extended. It doesn't respond easily to touch.

Hibernation is a good example of an unlearned response. The frog may have never hibernated before, yet it didn't have to be taught how to do it. All leopard frogs respond in the same way. Hibernation helps frogs to survive. They would starve or freeze during the cold winter unless they hibernated. A leopard frog can be made to hibernate any time during the year by reducing the temperature around it.

Take away the ice and let the water in the jar gradually warm up. Observe the changes that take place in the frog's behavior. As the water temperature rises, the frog will spend more time at the surface. Note the increase in breathing rate. How does the frog respond to touch and to light now?

8

Frogs In Nature

Like most small animals, frogs have a host of enemies. From egg to tadpole to adult frog, their life is not safe. Frogs may live for several years in a well-kept aquarium. In nature, from each bunch of thousands of eggs that are laid in the spring only a few frogs survive longer than one year.

Not only do water bugs, leeches, and flatworms eat frogs' eggs, but tadpoles and even mature frogs eat them. When the eggs hatch, there are more enemies waiting. One kind of water newt sometimes waits around an egg mass eating each tadpole as soon as it leaves the egg jelly.

Fish don't usually eat frogs' eggs, but seem to have a great appetite for tadpoles. Snakes, turtles, insects in their water stages, such as the dragonfly nymph and the water beetle, even certain kinds of spiders, share this appetite for tadpoles. But that's not all. Certain kinds of tadpoles eat smaller tadpoles. It's the rare tadpole that lives long enough to become a frog.

The adult frog has its own enemies. These include water snakes, garter snakes, black snakes, and any others that come upon a frog. Snapping turtles, musk turtles, and mud turtles eat their share. Birds such as herons, raccoons, weasels, skunks, cats, and dogs join in the hunt. Bullfrogs also enjoy eating smaller frogs.

Frogs don't have many defenses against their enemies. Perhaps their best defense is the way they look. When you see leopard frogs in an aquarium, it may be hard to believe that they are so difficult to see in nature. But place one in the grass, and their pattern of spots makes them almost invisible.

Frogs can jump great distances, of course. This helps in fleeing from enemies. Frogs also stiffen and remain motionless when an enemy is near. This helps them to escape notice.

Frogs scream when they are seized. The noise is not at all like their regular croak. The scream probably has little effect on an enemy, but may signal other frogs in the neighborhood, so that they have a better chance of escape.

But of all the enemies that frogs have, man may be the worst. Man kills frogs in many ways. Not only does man capture frogs, tadpoles, and eggs, but he

45

pollutes water with garbage, insect poisons, and sewerage. Man also drains swamps and fills them in, leaving less and less room for the natural life that abounds in these places.

Of what use are frogs? Some people eat frogs' legs, of course. Frogs are good insect eaters, and serve as food for larger animals such as fish and fur-bearing mammals. Many frogs are used in laboratories. They are certainly worth more to us alive than they are dead. But are these the only reasons for not killing frogs?

Of what use is a butterfly? Of what use is a quiet place in a field, or the rushing waters of a stream? Of what use is a summer evening in the country with the sounds of frogs croaking in the distance? Everything cannot be measured in terms of the money it is worth to man.

Perhaps frogs are not of much "use." But they are living animals, with interesting looks, and strange habits. All of us are still a part of the world of nature. Perhaps we can learn much about our own place in the natural world by studying the animals that share it with us.

46

~~~~~~

A Note on The Names of Frogs

COMMON NAMES	SCIENTIFIC NAMES
Meadow frog, Leopard frog	Rana pipiens
Pickerel frog, Spring frog	Rana palustis
Green frog	Rana clamitans
Bullfrog	Rana catesbeiana

47

Seymour Simon has been a science teacher for the last twelve years. He is a science book reviewer for *Scholastic Teacher Magazine*. He has served as a science consultant to Scholastic Magazine's *Summer Time* and was the science supplement writer for *NewsTime*. Scholastic Publications have published over fifty articles by Mr. Simon. In addition he has written juvenile science books, including *Animals in Field and Laboratory* and *Discovering What Earthworms Do*, which is part of this series. A native New Yorker, he was educated at City College, New York, and has done graduate work in psychology and biology. Mr. Simon lives at Great Neck, New York, with his wife and two boys.

Jean Zallinger has illustrated many children's books in the field of natural science; among these are *Valley of the Smallest, Ice Age, They Turned to Stone,* and *Discovering What Earthworms Do*. Mrs. Zallinger is a graduate of the Yale University Art Department. She now teaches art at a college in Connecticut. She and her husband have both illustrated for the *Life* "Epic of Man" series and for the "Time-Life Nature Libary" series. Mr. and Mrs. Zallinger have three children.